THE WAR FOR THE UNION.

A Lecture by Wendell Phillips, Esq., delivered in New York and Boston, December, 1861.—Revised by the Author.

REPORTED BY ANDREW J. GRAHAM.

Ladies and Gentlemen—It would be impossible for me fitly to thank you for this welcome; you will allow me, therefore, not to attempt it, but to avail myself of your patience to speak to you, as I have been invited to do, upon the war.

I know, ladies and gentlemen, that actions—deeds, not words—are the fitting duty of the hour. Yet, still, cannon think in this day of ours, and it is only by putting thought behind arms that we render them worthy, in any degree, of the civilization of the nineteenth century. [Applause.] Besides, the Government has two thirds of a million of soldiers, and it has ships sufficient for its purpose. The only question seems to be, what the Government is to do with these forces?—in what path, and how far it shall tread? You and I come here to-night, not to criticise, not to find fault with the Cabinet. We come here to recognize the fact, that in moments like these, the statesmanship of the Cabinet is but a pine shingle upon the rapids of Niagara, borne which way the great popular heart and the national purpose direct. It is in vain now, with these scenes about us, in this crisis, to endeavor to create public opinion; too late now to educate twenty million of people. Our object now is to concentrate and to manifest, to make evident and to make intense, the matured purpose of the nation. We are to show the world, if it be indeed so, that democratic institutions are strong enough for such an hour as this. Very terrible as is the conspiracy, momentous as is the peril, Democracy welcomes the struggle, confident that she stands like no delicately-poised throne in the Old World, but, like the pyramid, on its broadest base, able to be patient with national evils—generously patient with the long forbearance of three generations—and strong enough when, after that they reveal themselves in their own inevitable and hideous proportions, to pronounce and execute the unanimous verdict—Death!

Now, gentlemen, it is in such a spirit, with such a purpose, that I come before you to-night to sustain this war. Whence came this war? You and I need not curiously investigate. While Mr. Everett on one side, and Mr. Sumner on the other, agree, you and I may take for granted the opinion of two such opposite statesmen —the result of the common sense of this side of the water and the other—that slavery is the root of this war. [Applause.] I know some men have loved to trace it to disappointed ambition, to the success of the Republican party, convincing 300,000 nobles at the South, who have hitherto furnished us the most of the Presidents, Generals, Judges, and Ambassadors we needed, that they would have leave to stay at home, and that twenty million of Northerners would take their share in public affairs. I do not think that cause equal to the result. Other men before Jefferson Davis and Gov. Wise have been disappointed of the Presidency. Henry Clay, Daniel Webster, and Stephen A. Douglas were more than once disappointed, and yet who believes that either of these great men could have armed the North to avenge his wrongs? Why, then, should these pigmies of the South be able to do what the giants I have named could never achieve? Simply because there is a radical difference between the two sections, and that difference is slavery. A party victory may have been the *occasion* of this outbreak. So a tea-chest was the occasion of the Revolution, and it went to the bottom of Boston harbor on the night of the 16th of December, 1773; but that tea-chest was not the cause of the Revolution, neither is Jefferson Davis the cause of the rebellion. If you will look upon the map, and notice that every slave State has joined or tried to join the rebellion, and no free State has done so, I think you will not doubt substantially the origin of this convulsion.

Now, ladies and gentlemen, you know me—those of you who know me at all—simply as an Abolitionist. I am proud and glad that you should have known me as such. In the twenty-five years that are gone—I say it with no wish to offend any man before me —but in the quarter of a century that has passed, I could find no place where an American could stand with decent self-respect, except in constant, uncontrollable and loud protest against the sin of his native land. But, ladies and gentlemen, do not imagine that I come here to-night to speak simply and exclusively as an Abolitionist. My interest in this war, simply and exclusively as an Abolitionist, is about as much gone as yours in a novel where the hero has won the lady, and the marriage has been comfortably celebrated in the last chapter. I know the danger of political prophecy—a kaleidoscope of which not even a Yankee can guess the next combination—but for all that, I venture to offer my opinion, that on this continent the system of domestic slavery has received its death-blow. [Loud and long-continued applause.] Let me tell you why I think so. Leaving out of view war with England, which I do not expect, there are but three paths out of this war. One is, the North conquers; the other is, the South conquers; and the third is, a compromise. Now, if the North conquers, or there be a compromise, one or the other of two things must come—either the old Constitution or a new one. I believe that, so far as the slavery clauses of the Constitution of '89 are concerned, it is dead. It seems to me impossible that the thrifty and painstaking North, after keeping 600,000 men idle for two or three years, at a cost of two million dollars a day; after that flag lowered at Sumter; after Baker, and Lyon, and Ellsworth, and Winthrop, and Putnam, and Wesselhœft have given their lives to quell the rebellion; after our Massachusetts boys, hurrying from plowed field and workshop to save the capital, have been foully murdered on the pavements of Baltimore—I can not believe in a North so lost, so craven, as to put back slavery where it stood on the 4th of March last. [Cheers.] But if there be reconstruction without those slave clauses, then in a little while, longer or shorter, slavery dies—indeed, on any other basis but the basis of '89, she has nothing else now to do but to die. On the contrary, if the South —no, I can not say conquers—my lips will not form that word— but if she balks us of victory, the only way she can do it is to write Emancipation on her own banner, and thus bribe the friends of liberty in Europe to allow its aristocrats and traders to divide the majestic Republic whose growth and trade they fear and envy. Either way the slave goes free. Unless England flings her fleets along the coast, the South can never spring into separate existence, except from the basis of negro freedom; and I, for one, can not yet believe that the North will consent again to share his chains. Exclusively, as an Abolitionist, therefore, I have little more interest in this war than the frontiersman's wife had in his struggle with the bear, when she didn't care which whipped. But before I leave the Abolitionists, let me say one word. Some men say we are the cause of this war. Gentlemen, you do us too much honor! If it be so, we have reason to be proud of it; for in my heart, as an American, I believe this year the most glorious of the Republic since '76. The North, craven and contented until now, like Mammon, saw nothing even in heaven but the golden pavement; to-day she throws off her chains. We have a North, as Daniel Webster said. This is no epoch for nations to blush at. England might blush in 1620, when Englishmen trembled at a fool's frown, and were silent when James forbade them to think; but not in 1649, when an outraged people cut off his son's head. Massachusetts might have blushed a year or two ago, when an insolent Virginian, standing on Bunker Hill, insulted the Commonwealth, and then dragged her citizens to Washington to tell what they knew about John Brown; but she has no reason to blush to-day, when she holds that same impudent Senator an acknowledged felon in her prison fort. In my view, the bloodiest war ever waged is infinitely better than the happiest slavery that ever fattened men into obedience. And yet I love peace. But it is real peace; not peace such as we have had; not peace that meant lynch law in the Carolinas and mob law in New York; not peace that meant chains around Boston Court-House, a gag on the lips of statesmen, and the slave sobbing himself to sleep in curses. No more such peace for me; no peace that is not born of justice, and does not recognize the rights of every race and every man.

Some men say they would view this war as white men. I condescend to no such narrowness. I view it as an American citizen, proud to be the citizen of an empire that knows neither black nor white, neither Saxon nor Indian, but holds an equal scepter over all. [Loud cheers.] If I am to love my country, it must be lovable; if I am to honor it, it must be worthy of respect. What is the function God gives us—what is the breadth of responsibility he lays upon us? An empire, the home of every race, every creed, every tongue, to whose citizens is committed, if not the only, then the grandest system of pure self-government. De Tocqueville tells us that all nations and all ages tend with inevitable certainty to this result, but he points out, as history does, this land as the normal school of the nations, set by God to try the experiment of popular education and popular government, to remove the obstacles, point out the dangers, find the best way, encourage the timid, and hasten the world's progress. Let us see to it, that with such a crisis and such a past, neither the ignorance, nor the heedlessness, nor the cowardice of Americans forfeits this high honor, won for us by the toils of two generations, given to us by the blessing of Providence. It is as a citizen of the leading State of this Western Continent, vast in territory, and yet its territory nothing when compared with the grandeur of its past and the majesty of its future—it is as such a citizen that I wish, for one, to find out my duty, express as an individual my opinion, and aid thereby the Cabinet in doing its duty under such responsibility. It does not lie in one man to ruin us, nor in one man to save us, nor in a dozen. It lies in the twenty million, in the thirty million, of thirty-four States.

Now, how do we stand? In a war—not only that, but a terrific war—not a war sprung from the caprice of a woman, the spite of a priest, the flickering ambition of a prince, as wars usually have; but a war inevitable; in one sense, nobody's fault; the inevitable result of past training, the conflict of ideas, millions of people grappling each other's throats, every soldier in each camp certain that he is fighting for an idea that holds the salvation of the world—every drop of his blood in earnest. Such a war finds no parallel nearer than that of the Catholic and the Huguenot of France, or than that of Aristocrat and Republican in 1790, or of Cromwell and the Irish, when victory meant extermination. Such is our war. I look upon it as the commencement of the great struggle between the hidden aristocracy and the democracy of America. You are to say to-day whether it shall last ten years or seventy, as it usually has done. It resembles closely that struggle between aristocrat and democrat which began in France in 1790, and continues still. While it lasts, it will have the same effect on the nation as that war between blind loyalty, represented by the Stuart family, and the free spirit of the English Constitution, which lasted from 1660 to 1760, and made England a second-rate power almost all that century.

Such is the era on which you are entering. I will not speak of war in itself—I have no time; I will not say with Napoleon that it is the practice of barbarians; I will not say that it is good. It is better than the past. A thing may be *better*, and yet not *good*. This war is better than the past, but there is not an element of good in it. I mean, there is nothing in it that we might not have gotten better, fuller, and more perfectly in other ways. And yet it is better than the craven past, infinitely better than a peace which had pride for its father and subserviency for its mother. Neither will I speak of the cost of war, although you know that we never shall get out of this one without a debt of at least two or three thousand million of dollars. For, if the prevalent theory prove correct, and the country comes together again on anything like the old basis, we pay Jeff Davis' debts as well as our own.

Neither will I remind you that debt is the fatal disease of republics, the first thing and the mightiest to undermine government and corrupt the people. The great debt of England has kept her back in civil progress at least a hundred years. Neither will I remind you that when we go out of this war, we go out with an immense disbanded army, an intense military spirit embodied in two thirds of a million of soldiers, the fruitful, the inevitable source of fresh debts and new wars: I pass by all that; yet lying within those causes are things enough to make the most sanguine friends of free institutions tremble for our future. I pass those by. But let me remind you of another tendency of the time. You know, for instance, that the writ of *habeas corpus*, by which government is bound to render a reason to the judiciary before it lays its hands upon a citizen, has been called the high-water mark of English liberty. Jefferson, in his calm moments, dreaded the power to suspend it in any emergency whatever, and wished to have it in "eternal and unremitting force." The present Napoleon, in his treatise on the English Constitution, calls it the gem of English institutions. Lieber says that *habeas corpus*, free meetings like this, and a free press, are the three elements which distinguish liberty from despotism. All that Saxon blood has gained in the battles and toils of two hundred years are these three things. But to-day, Mr. Chairman, every one of them—*habeas corpus*, the right of free meeting, and a free press—is annihilated in every square mile of the Republic. We live to-day, every one of us, under martial law. The Secretary of State puts into his bastile, with a warrant as irresponsible as that of Louis, any man whom he pleases. And you know that neither press nor lips may venture to arraign the Government without being silenced. At this moment one thousand men, at least, are "bastiled" by an authority as despotic as that of Louis—three times as many as Eldon and George III. seized when they trembled for his throne. Mark me, I am not complaining. I do not say it is not necessary. It is necessary to do anything to save the ship. [Applause.] It is necessary to throw everything overboard in order that we may float. It is a mere question whether you prefer the despotism of Washington or that of Richmond. I prefer that of Washington. [Loud applause.] But, nevertheless, I point out to you this tendency because it is momentous in its significance. We are tending with rapid strides, you say *inevitably*—I do not deny it; *necessarily*—I do not question it; we are tending toward that strong government which frightened Jefferson; toward that unlimited debt, that endless army. We have already those alien and sedition laws which, in 1798, wrecked the Federal party, and summoned the Democratic into existence. For the first time on this continent, we have passports, which even Louis Napoleon pronounces useless and odious. For the first time in our history, government spies frequent our great cities. And this model of a strong government, if you reconstruct it on the old basis, is to be handed into the keeping of whom? If you compromise it by reconstruction, to whom are you to give these delicate and grave powers? To compromisers. Reconstruct this Government, and for twenty years you can never elect a Republican. Presidents must be so wholly without character or principle, that two angry parties, each hopeless of success, contemptuously tolerate them as neutrals. Now, I am not exaggerating the moment. I can parallel it entirely. It is the same position that England held in the times of Eldon and Fox, when Holcroft and Montgomery, the poet, Horne Tooke and Frost and Hardy went into dungeons, under laws that Pitt executed and Burke praised—times when Fox said he despaired of English liberty but for the power of insurrection—times which Sydney Smith said he remembered, when no man was entitled to an opinion who had not £3,000 a year. Why! there is no right—do I exaggerate when I say that there is no single right—that government is scrupulous and finds itself able to protect, except the pretended right of a man to his slaves! Every other right has fallen now before the necessities of the hour.

Understand me, I do not complain of this state of things; but it is momentous. I only ask you that out of this peril you be sure to get something worthy of the crisis through which you have passed. No government of free make could stand three such trials as this. I only paint you the picture, in order, like Hotspur, to say, "Out of this nettle, danger, be you right eminently sure that you pluck the flower, safety." [Applause.] Standing in such a crisis, certainly it commands us that we should endeavor to find the root of the difficulty, and that now, once for all, we should put it beyond the possibility of troubling our peace again. We can not afford, as Republicans, to run that risk. The vessel of state—her timbers are strained beyond almost the possibility of surviving. The tempest is one which it demands the wariest pilot to outlive. We can not afford, thus warned, to omit anything which can save this ship of state from a second danger of the kind.

Well, what shall we do? The answer to that question comes partly from what we think has been the cause of this convulsion. Some men think—some of your editors think—many of ours, too—that this war is nothing but the disappointment of one or two thousand angered politicians, who have persuaded eight million of Southerners, against their convictions, to take up arms and rush to the battle-field—no great compliment to Southern sense. [Laughter.] They think that if the Federal army could only appear in the midst of this demented mass, the eight million will find out for the first time in their lives that they have got souls of their own, tell us so, and then we shall all be piloted back, float back, drift back into the good old times of Franklin Pierce and James Buchanan. [Laughter.] Well, there is a measure of truth in that. I believe that if a year ago, when the thing first showed itself, Jefferson Davis, and Toombs, and Keitt, and Wise, and the rest, had been hung for traitors at Washington, and a couple of frigates anchored at Charleston, another couple in Savannah, and half a dozen in New Orleans, with orders to shell those cities on the first note of resistance, there never would have been this outbreak—[applause]—or it would have been postponed at least a dozen years; and if that interval had been used to get rid of slavery, we never should have heard of the convulsion. But you know we had nothing of the kind, and the consequence is, what? Why, the bewildered North has been summoned by every defeat, and every success, from its workshops and its factories, to gaze with half-opened eyes at the lurid heavens, until at last, divided, bewildered, confounded, as this 20,000,000 were, we have all of us fused into one idea, that the Union meant Justice—shall mean Justice—owns down to the Gulf, and we will have it. [Applause.] Well, what has taken place meanwhile at the South? Why, the same thing. The divided, bewildered South has been summoned also out of her divisions by every success and every defeat (and she has had more of the first than we have), and the consequence is that she, too, is fused into a swelling sea of state pride, Northern hate—

> "Unconquerable will,
> And study of revenge, immortal hate,
> And courage never to submit nor yield."

She is in earnest, every man, and she is as unanimous as the Colonies were in the Revolution. In fact, the South recognizes more intelligibly than we do the necessities of her position. I do not consider this a secession. It is no secession. I agree with Bishop-

General Polk—it is a conspiracy, not a secession. There is no wish, no intention to go peaceably and permanently off. It is a conspiracy to make the Government do the will and accept the policy of the slaveholders. Its root is at the South, but it has many a branch in Wall Street and in State Street. [Cheers.] It is a conspiracy, and on the one side is every man who still thinks that he that steals his brother is a gentleman, and he that makes his living is not. [Applause.] It is the aristocratic element which survived the Constitution, which our fathers thought could be left under it, and the South to-day is forced into this war by the natural growth of the antagonistic principle. You may pledge whatever submission and patience of Southern institutions you please, it is not enough. South Carolina said to Massachusetts, in 1835, when Edward Everett was Governor, "Abolish free speech—it is a nuisance." She is right—from her stand-point it is. [Laughter.] That is, it is not possible to preserve the quiet of South Carolina consistently with free speech; but you know the story Sir Walter Scott told of the Scotch laird, who said to his old butler, "Jock, you and I can't live under this roof." "And where does your honor think of going?" So free speech says to South Carolina to-day. Now I say you may pledge, compromise, guarantee what you please. The South knows it is not your purpose—it is your character that she dreads. It is the nature of Northern institutions, the perilous freedom of discussion, the flavor of our ideas, the sight of our growth, the very neighborhood of such States, that constitutes the danger. It is like the two vases launched on the stormy sea. The iron said to the crockery, "I wont come near you." "Thank you," said the weaker vessel; "there is as much danger in my coming near you." This the South feels; hence her determination; hence, indeed, the imperious necessity that she should rule and shape our Government, or of sailing out of it. I do not mean that she plans to take possession of the North, and choose our Northern mayors, though she has done that in Boston for the last dozen years, and here till this fall. But she conspires and aims to control just so much of our policy, trade, offices, presses, pulpits, cities, as is sufficient to insure the undisturbed existence of slavery. She conspires with the full intent so to mold this Government as to keep it what it has been for thirty years, according to John Quincy Adams—a plot for the extension and perpetuation of slavery. As the world advances, fresh guarantees are demanded. The nineteenth century requires sterner gags than the eighteenth. Often as the peace of Virginia is in danger, you must be willing that a Virginia Mason shall drag your citizens to Washington, and imprison them at his pleasure. So long as Carolina needs it, you must submit that your ships be searched for dangerous passengers, and every Northern man lynched. No more Kansas rebellions. It is a conflict between the two powers, Aristocracy and Democracy, *which shall hold this belt of the continent.* You may live here, New York men, but it must be in submission to such rules as the quiet of Carolina requires. That is the meaning of the oft-repeated threat to call the roll of one's slaves on Bunker Hill, and dictate peace in Faneuil Hall. Now, in that fight, I go for the North—for the Union.

In order to make out this theory of "irrepressible conflict," it is not necessary to suppose that every Southerner hates every Northerner (as the *Atlantic* urges). But this much is true, some 300,000 slaveholders at the South, holding two thousand million of so-called property in their hands, controlling the blacks, and befooling the seven million of poor whites into being their tools, into believing their interest is opposed to ours—this order of nobles, this privileged class, has been able for forty years to keep the Government in dread, dictate terms by threatening disunion, bring us to its verge at least twice, and now almost to break the Union in pieces. A power thus consolidated, which has existed seventy years, setting up and pulling down parties, controlling the policy of the Government, and changing our religion, and is emboldened by uniform success, will not burst like a bubble in an hour. For all practical purposes, it is safe to speak of it as the South; no other South exists, or will exist, till our policy develops it into being. This is what I mean. An aristocracy rooted in wealth, with its network spread over all social life, its poison penetrating every fiber of society, is the hardest possible evil to destroy. Its one influence, FASHION, is often able to mock at Religion, Trade, Literature, and Politics combined. One half the reason why Washington has been and is in peril—why every move is revealed and checkmated—is that your President is unfashionable, and Mrs. Jefferson Davis is not. Unseen chains are sometimes stronger than those of iron and heavier than those of gold.

It is not in the plots, it is in the inevitable character of the Northern States that the South sees her danger. And the struggle is between these two ideas. Our fathers, as I said, thought they could be left, one to outgrow the other. They took gunpowder and a lighted match, forced them into a stalwart cannon, screwed down the muzzle, and thought they could secure peace. But it has resulted differently, their cannon has exploded, and we stand among fragments.

Now some Republicans and some Democrats—not Butler, and Bryant, and Cochrane, and Cameron, not Boutwell, and Bancroft, and Dickinson, and others—but the old set—the old set say to the Republicans, "Lay the pieces carefully together in their places; put the gunpowder and the match in again, say the Constitution backward instead of your prayers, and there will never be another rebellion!" Now I doubt it. It seems to me that like causes will produce like effects. If the reason of the war is because we are two nations, then the cure must be to make us one nation, to remove that cause which divides us, to make our institutions homogeneous. If it were possible to subjugate the South and leave slavery where it is, where is the security that we should not have another war in ten years? Indeed, such a course invites another war, whenever demagogues please. I believe the policy of reconstruction is impossible. And if it were possible, it would be the greatest mistake that Northern men could commit. [Cheers.] I will not stop to remind you that, standing as we do to-day, with the full constitutional right to abolish slavery—a right Southern treason has just given us—a right, the use of which is enjoined by the sternest necessity—if, after that, the North goes back to the Constitution of '89, she assumes, a second time, afresh, unnecessarily, a criminal responsibility for slavery. Hereafter no old excuse will avail us. A second time, with open eyes, against our highest interest, we clasp bloody hands with tyrants to uphold an acknowledged sin, whose fell evil we have fully proved.

But that aside, peace with an unchanged Constitution would leave us to stand like Mexico. States married, not matched; chained together, not melted into one; foreign nations aware of our hostility, and interfering to embroil, rob, and control us. We should be what Greece was under the intrigues of Philip, and Germany when Louis XIV. was in fact her dictator. We may see our likeness in Austria, every fretful province an addition of weakness; in Italy, twenty years ago, a leash of angry hounds. A Union with unwilling and subjugated States, smarting with defeat, and yet holding the powerful and dangerous element of slavery in it, and an army disbanded into laborers, food for constant disturbance, would be a standing invitation to France and England to insult and dictate, to thwart our policy, demand changes in our laws, and trample on us continually.

Reconstruction is but another name for the submission of the North. It is her subjection under a mask. It is nothing but the confession of defeat. Every merchant, in such a case, puts everything he has at the bidding of Wigfall and Toombs in every crossroad bar-room at the South. For, you see, never till now did anybody but a few Abolitionists believe that this nation could be marshaled one section against the other in arms. But the secret is out. The weak point is discovered. Why does the London press lecture us like a schoolmaster his seven-years-old boy? Why does England use a tone such as she has not used for half a century to any power? Because she knows us as she knows Mexico, as all Europe knows Austria—that we have the cancer concealed in our very vitals. Slavery, left where it is, after having created such a war as this, would leave our commerce and all our foreign relations at the mercy of any Keitt, Wigfall, Wise, or Toombs. Any demagogue has only to stir up a pro-slavery crusade, point back to the safe experiment of 1861, and lash the passions of the aristocrats to cover the sea with privateers, put in jeopardy the trade of twenty States, plunge the country into millions of debt, send our stocks down fifty per cent., and cost thousands of lives. Reconstruction is but making chronic what now is transient. What that is, this week shows. What that is, we learn from the tone England dares to assume toward this divided republic. I do not believe reconstruction possible. I do not believe the Cabinet intend it. True, I should care little if they did, since I believe the administration can no more resist the progress of events than a spear of grass can retard the step of an avalanche. But if they do, allow me to say, for one, that every dollar spent in this war is worse than wasted, every life lost is a public murder, and that any statesman who leads these States back to reconstruction will be damned to an infamy compared with which Arnold was a saint, and James Buchanan a public benefactor. [Slight disturbance in the rear part of the hall, cries of "Put him out!" etc.] I said reconstruction is not possible. I do not believe it is, for this reason: the moment these States begin to appear victorious, the moment our armies do anything that evinces final success, the wily statesmanship and unconquerable hate of the South will write "Emancipation" on her banner, and welcome the protectorate of a European power. And if you read the European papers of to-day, you need not doubt that they will have it. Intelligent men agree that the North stands better with Palmerston for minister than she would with any minister likely to succeed him. And who is Palmerston? While he was Foreign Secretary, from 1848 to '51, the British press ridiculed every effort of the French Republicans—sneered at Cavaignac and Ledru Rollin, Lamartine and Hugo—while they cheered Napoleon on to his usurpation; and Lord Normanby, then minister at Paris, early in December, while Napoleon's hand was still wet with the best blood of France, congratulated the despot on his victory over the Reds, applying to the friends of Liberty the worst epithet that an Englishman knows. This last outrage lost Palmerston his place; but he rules to-day—though rebuked, not changed.

The value of the English news this week is the indication of the nation's mind. No one doubts now, that should the South emancipate, England would make haste to recognize and help her. In ordinary times the Government and aristocracy of England dread American example. They may well admire and envy the strength of our Government, when, instead of England's impressment and pinched levies, patriotism marshals six hundred thousand *volunteers* in six months. The English merchant is jealous of our growth; only the liberal middle classes really sympathize with us. When the two other classes are divided, this middle class rules. But now, Herod and Pilate are agreed. The aristocrat, who usually despises a trader, whether of Manchester or Liverpool, as the South does a negro, now is secessionist from sympathy, as the trader is from interest. Such a union no middle class can checkmate. The only danger of war with England is, that as soon as England declared war with us, she would recognize the Southern Confederacy immediately, just as she stands, slavery and all, as a military measure. As such, in the heat of passion, in the smoke of war, the English people, all of them, would allow such a recognition even of a slaveholding empire. War with England insures disunion. When England declares war, she gives slavery a fresh lease of fifty years. Even if we have no war with England, let another eight or ten months be as little successful as the last, and Europe will acknowledge the Southern Confederacy, slavery and all, as a matter of course. Further, any approach toward victory on our part, without freeing the slave, gives him free to Davis. So far, the South is sure to succeed, either by victory or defeat, unless we anticipate her. Indeed, the only way, the only sure way, to break this Union, is to try to save it by protecting slavery. "Every moment lost," as Napoleon said, "is an opportunity for misfortune." Unless we emancipate the slave, we shall never conquer the South without her trying emancipation. Every Southerner, from Toombs up to Fremont, has acknowledged it. Do you suppose that Davis and Beauregard, and the rest, mean to be exiles, wandering contemned in every great city of Europe, in order that they may maintain slavery and the Constitution of '89? They, like ourselves, will throw everything overboard before they will submit to defeat—defeat from Yankees. I do not believe, therefore, that reconciliation is possible, nor do I believe the Cabinet have any such hopes. Indeed, I do not know where you will find the evidence of *any* purpose in the administration at Washington. [Hisses, cheers, and laughter.] If we look to the West, if we look to the Potomac, what is the policy? If, on the Potomac, with the aid of twenty governors, you assemble an army, and do nothing but return fugitive slaves, that proves you competent and efficient. If, on the banks of the Mississippi, unaided, the magic of your presence summons an army into existence, and you drive your enemy before you a hundred miles farther than your second in command thought it possible for you to advance, that proves you incompetent, and entitles your second in command to succeed you. [Tremendous applause, and three cheers for Fremont!]

Looking in another direction, you see the Government announcing a policy in South Carolina. What is it? Well, Mr. Secretary Cameron says to the General in command there, "You are to welcome into your camp all comers; you are to organize them into squads and companies; use them any way you please—but there is to be no general arming." That is a very significant exception. You recollect in Charles Reade's novel, "Never too Late to Mend" (a very good motto), the heroine flies away to hide from the hero, announcing that she never shall see him again. Her letter says, "I will never see you again, Edward. You, of course, won't come to see me at Mrs. Young's, at No. 126 Bond Street—[laughter]—between eleven in the morning and four in the afternoon, because I shan't see you." [Laughter.] So Mr. Cameron says there is to be no general arming, but I suppose there is to be a very particular arming. [Laughter.] But he goes on to add: "This is no greater interference with the institutions of South Carolina than is necessary—than the war will cure." Does he mean he will give the slaves back when the war is over? I don't know. All I know is, that the Port Royal expedition proved one thing—it laid forever that ghost of an argument, that the blacks loved their masters—it settled forever the question whether the blacks were with us or with the South. My opinion is, that the blacks are the key of our position. [A VOICE—"That is it."] He that gets them wins, and he that loses them goes to the wall. [Applause.] Port Royal settled one thing—the blacks are with us, and not with the South. At present they are the only Unionists. I know nothing more touching in history, nothing that art will immortalize and poetry dwell upon more fondly—I know no tribute to the stars and stripes more impressive than that incident of the blacks coming to the water side with their little bundles, in that simple faith which had endured through the long night of so many bitter years. They preferred to be shot rather than be driven from the sight of that banner they had so long prayed to see. And if that was the result when nothing but Gen. Sherman's equivocal proclamation was landed on the Carolinas, what should we have seen, if there had been 18,000 veterans with Fremont, the statesman soldier of this war, at their head—[loud applause]—and over them the stars and stripes, gorgeous with the motto, "Freedom for all! freedom forever?" If that had gone before them, in my opinion they would have marched across the Carolinas, and joined Brownlow in East Tennessee. [Applause.] The bulwark on each side of them would have been 100,000 grateful blacks; they would have cut this rebellion in halves, and while our fleets fired salutes across New Orleans, Beauregard would have been ground to powder between the upper millstone of McClellan, and the lower of a quarter million of blacks rising to greet the stars and stripes. [Great cheering.] McClellan may drill a better army—more perfect soldiers. He will never marshal a stronger force than those grateful thousands. That is the way to save insurrection. He is an enemy to civil liberty, the worst enemy to his own land, who asks for such delay or perversion of Government policy as is sure to result in insurrection. Our duty is to save these four millions of blacks from their own passions, from their own confusion, and eight million of whites from the consequences of it—["Hear, hear!"]—and in order to do it, we nineteen million of educated, Christian Americans are not to wait for the will or the wisdom of a single man—we are not to wait for Fremont or McClellan—the Government is our dictator. It might do for Rome, a herd of beggars and soldiers, kept quiet only by the weight of despotism—it might do for Rome, in moments of danger, to hurl all responsibility into the hands of a dictator. But for us, educated, thoughtful men, with institutions modeled and matured by the experience of two hundred years—it is not for us to evade responsibility by deferring to a single man. I demand of the Government a policy. I demand of the Government to show the doubting infidels of Europe that Democracy is not only strong enough for the trial, but that she breeds men with brains large enough to comprehend the hour, and wills hot enough to fuse the purpose of nineteen million of people into one decisive blow for safety and for Union. [Cheers.] You will ask me how it is to be done. I would have it done by Congress. We have the power.

When Congress declares war, says John Quincy Adams, Congress has all the powers incident to carrying on war.* It is not an unconstitutional power—it is a power conferred by the Constitution—but the moment it comes into play it rises beyond the limit of constitutional checks. I know it is a grave power, this trusting the Government with despotism. But what is the use of government, except just to help us in critical times? All the checks and ingenuity of our institutions are arranged to secure for us men wise and able enough to be trusted with grave powers—bold enough to use them when the times require. Lancets and knives are dangerous instruments. The use of surgeons is, that when lancets are needed somebody may know how to use them, and save

* "Sir, in the authority given to Congress by the Constitution of the United States to *declare war*, ALL THE POWERS INCIDENTAL TO WAR are, by necessary implication, conferred upon the GOVERNMENT of the United States. . . . . There are two classes of powers vested by the Constitution of the United States in their Congress and Executive government: the powers to be executed in time of peace, and the powers incident to war. That the powers of peace are limited by provisions within the body of the Constitution itself; but that the powers of war are limited and regulated only by the laws and usages of nations, and are subject to no other limitation. . . . . I do not admit that there is, *even among the peace powers of Congress*, no such authority; but IN WAR, there are many ways by which CONGRESS NOT ONLY HAVE THE AUTHORITY, BUT ARE BOUND TO INTERFERE WITH THE INSTITUTION OF SLAVERY IN THE STATES. . . . . When the Southern States are the battle-field between Slavery and Emancipation, Congress may sustain the institution by war, or perhaps ABOLISH IT BY treaties of peace; and they will not only possess the constitutional power so to interfere, but THEY WILL BE BOUND IN DUTY TO DO IT, *by the express provisions of the Constitution itself.* From the instant the slaveholding States become the theater of a war, *civil, servile, or foreign*, from that instant *the war powers of Congress extend to interference with the institution of slavery* IN EVERY WAY BY WHICH IT CAN BE INTERFERED WITH. . . . . With a call to keep down slaves, in an insurrection and a civil war, comes a full and plenary power *to this House* and *to the Senate* over the whole subject. It is a war power. Whether it be a war of invasion or a war of insurrection, Congress has power to carry on the war, and must carry it on, according to the laws of war; and by the laws of war an invaded country has all its laws and municipal institutions *swept by the board*, and martial law takes the place of them. This *power in Congress* has, perhaps, never been called into exercise under the present Constitution of the United States."—*Speeches of John Quincy Adams in the U. S. House of Representatives*, 1836–1842.

life. One great merit of democratic institutions is, that resting, as they must, on educated masses, the Government may safely be trusted, in a great emergency, with despotic power, without fear of harm, or of wrecking the state. No other form of government can venture such confidence without risk of national ruin. Doubtless the war power is a very grave power; so are some ordinary peace powers. I will not cite extreme cases, Louisiana and Texas. We obtained the first by Treaty, the second by Joint Resolutions; each case an exercise of power as grave and despotic as the abolition of slavery would be, and, unlike that, plainly unconstitutional; one which nothing but stern necessity and subsequent acquiescence by the nation could make valid. Let me remind you that seventy years' practice has incorporated it as a principle in our constitutional law, that what the necessity of the hour demands and continued assent of the people ratifies is law. Slavery has established that rule. We might surely use it in the cause of justice. But I will cite an unquestionable precedent. It was a grave power, in 1807, in time of peace, when Congress abolished commerce; when, by the embargo of Jefferson, no ship could quit New York or Boston, and Congress set no limit to the prohibition. It annihilated commerce. New England asked, "Is it constitutional?" The Supreme Court said, "Yes." New England sat down and obeyed. Her wharves were worthless, her ships rotted, her merchants beggared. She asked no compensation. The powers of Congress carried bankruptcy from New Haven to Portland; but the Supreme Court said, "It is legal," and New England bowed her head. We commend the same cup to the Carolinas to-day. We say to them that, in order to save the Government, there resides somewhere despotism. It is in the war powers of Congress. That despotism can change the social arrangements of the Southern States, and has a right to do it. Every man of you who speaks of the emancipation of the negroes, allows it would be decisive if it were used. You allow that, when it is a military necessity, we may use it. What I claim is, in honor of our institutions, that we are not put to wait for the wisdom or the courage of a General, Our fathers left us with no such miserable plan of government. They gave us a government with the power, in such times as these of doing something that would save the helm of state in the hands of its citizens. [Cheers.] We could cede the Carolinas; I have sometimes wished we could shovel them into the Atlantic. [Applause and laughter.] We can cede a State. We can do anything for the time being; and no theory of government can deny its power to make the most unlimited change. The only alternative is this: Do you prefer the despotism of your own citizens or of foreigners? That is the only question in war. [Cheers.]

Now, this Government, which abolishes my right of *habeas corpus*—which strikes down, because it is necessary, every Saxon bulwark of liberty—which proclaims martial law, and holds every dollar and every man at the will of the Cabinet—do you turn round and tell me that this same Government has no power to stretch its hands across the Potomac, and root up the evil which, for seventy years, has troubled its peace, and now culminates in rebellion? I maintain, therefore, the power of the Government itself to inaugurate a policy; and I say, in order to save the Union, do justice to the black. [Applause.]

I would claim of Congress—in the exact language of Adams, of the "*Government*"—a solemn act abolishing slavery throughout the Union, securing compensation to loyal slaveholders. As the Constitution forbids the States to make and allow nobles, I would now, by equal authority, forbid them to make slaves or allow slaveholders.

This has been the usual course at such times. Nations, convulsed and broken by two powerful elements or institutions, have used the first moment of assured power—the first moment that they clearly saw and fully appreciated the evil—to cut up the dangerous tree by the roots. So France expelled the Jesuits, and the Middle Ages the Templars. So England, in her great rebellion, abolished Nobility and the Established Church; and the French Revolution did the same, and finally gave to each child an equal share in his deceased father's lands. For the same purpose, England, in 1745, abolished clanship in Scotland, the root of the Stuart faction; and we, in '76, nobles and all tenure of estates savoring of privileged classes. Such a measure supplies the South just what she needs—capital. That sum which the North gives the loyal slaveholder, not as acknowledging his property in the slave, but a measure of conciliation—perhaps an acknowledgment of its share of the guilt—will call mills, ships, agriculture into being. The free negro will redeem to use lands never touched, whose fertility laughs Illinois to scorn, and finds no rival but Egypt. And remember, besides, as Montesquieu says, "The yield of land depends less on its fertility than on the freedom of its inhabitants." Such a measure binds the negro to us by the indissoluble tie of gratitude—the loyal slaveholder by strong self-interest—our bonds are all his property—the other whites, by prosperity, they are lifted in the scale of civilization and activity, educated and enriched. Our institutions are then homogeneous. We grapple the Union together with hooks of steel—make it as lasting as the granite that underlies the continent.

People may say this is a strange language for me—a Disunionist. Well, I was a Disunionist, sincerely, for twenty years. I did hate the Union, when Union meant lies in the pulpit and mobs in the street, when Union meant making white men hypocrites and black men slaves. [Cheers.] I did prefer purity to peace—I acknowledge it. The child of six generations of Puritans, knowing well the value of union, I did prefer disunion to being the accomplice of tyrants. But now, when I see what the Union must mean in order to last—when I see that you can not have union without meaning justice—and when I see twenty millions of people, with a current as swift and as inevitable as Niagara, determined that this Union shall mean justice, why should I object to it? I endeavored honestly, and am not ashamed of it, to take nineteen States out of this Union, and consecrate them to liberty, and twenty millions of people answer me back, "We like your motto, only we mean to keep thirty-four States under it." Do you suppose I am not Yankee enough to buy union when I can have it at a fair price? I know the value of union; and the reason why I claim that Carolina has no right to secede is this: we are not a partnership, we are a marriage, and we have done a great many things since we were married in 1789 which render it unjust for a State to exercise the right of revolution on any ground now alleged. I admit the right. I acknowledge the great principles of the Declaration of Independence, that a State exists for the liberty and happiness of the people, that these are the ends of government, and that when government ceases to promote those ends, the people have a right to remodel their institutions. I acknowledge the right of revolution in South Carolina, but at the same time I acknowledge that right of revolution only when Government has ceased to promote those ends. Now we have been married for seventy years. We have bought Florida. We rounded the Union to the Gulf. We bought the Mississippi for commercial purposes. We bought Texas for slave purposes. Great commercial interests, great interests of peace have been subserved by rounding the Union into a perfect shape; and the money and sacrifices of two generations have been given for this purpose. To break up that Union now is to defraud us of mutual advantages relating to peace, trade, national security, which can not survive disunion. The right of revolution is not matter of caprice. "Governments long established," says our Declaration of Independence, "are not to be changed for light and transient causes." When so many important interests and benefits, in their nature indivisible and which disunion destroys, have been secured by common toils and cost, the South must vindicate her revolution by showing that our Government has become destructive of its proper ends, else the right of revolution does not exist. Why did we buy Texas? Why have we allowed the South to strengthen herself? Because she said that slavery within the girdle of the Constitution would die out through the influence of natural principles. She said: "We acknowledge it to be an evil; but at the same time it will end by the spread of free principles and the influence of free institutions." And the North said: "Yes; we will give you privileges on that account, and we will return your slaves for you." Every slave sent back from a Northern State is a fresh oath of the South that she would not secede. Our fathers trusted to the promise that this race should be left under the influence of the Union, until, in the maturity of time, the day should arrive when they would be lifted into the sunlight of God's equality. I claim it of South Carolina. By virtue of that pledge she took Boston, and put a rope round her neck in that infamous compromise which consigned to slavery Anthony Burns. I demand the fulfillment on her part even of that infamous pledge. Until South Carolina allows me all the influence that nineteen millions of Yankee lips, asking infinite questions, have upon the welfare of those four million of bondsmen, I deny her right to secede. [Applause.] Seventy years has the Union postponed the negro. For seventy years has he been beguiled with the promise, as she erected one bulwark after another around slavery, that he should have the influence of our common institutions. I claim it to-day. Never, with my consent, while the North thinks that the Union can or shall mean justice, shall those 400,000 South Carolina slaves go beyond the influence of Boston ideas. That is my strong reason for clinging to the Union. This is also one main reason why, unless upon most *imperative* and *manifest* grounds of need and right, South Carolina has no right of revolution; none till she fulfills her promise in this respect.

I know how we stand to-day, with the frowning cannon of the English fleet ready to be thrust out of the port-holes against us.

But I can answer England with a better answer than William H. Seward can write. I can answer her with a more statesmanlike paper than Simon Cameron can indite. I would answer her with the stars and stripes floating over Charleston and New Orleans, and the itinerant Cabinet of Richmond packing up archives and wearing apparel to ride back to Montgomery. There is one thing, and only one, that John Bull respects, and that is success. It is not for us to give counsel to the Government on points of diplomatic propriety; but I suppose we may express our opinion, and my opinion is, that if I were the President of these thirty-four States, while I was, I should want Mason and Slidell to stay with me. I say, then, first, as a matter of justice to the slave, we owe it to him; the day of his deliverance has come. The long promise of seventy years is to be fulfilled. The South draws back from the pledge. The North is bound, in honor of the memory of her fathers, to demand its exact fulfillment, and in order to save this Union, which now means justice and peace, to recognize the rights of 4,000,000 of its victims. This is the dictate of Justice. Justice, which at this hour is craftier than Seward, more statesmanlike than Cameron; Justice, which appeals from the cabinets of Europe to the people; Justice, which abases the proud and lifts up the humble; Justice, which disarms England, saves the slaves from insurrection, and sends home the Confederate army of the Potomac to guard its own hearths; Justice, which gives us four million of friends, spies, soldiers in the enemy's country, planted each one at their very hearth-sides; Justice, which inscribes every cannon with "Holiness to the Lord!" and puts a Northern heart behind every musket; Justice, which means victory now and peace forever. To all cry of demagogues asking for boldness, I respond with the cry of "Justice, immediate, absolute Justice!" And if I dared to descend to a lower level, I should say to the merchants of this metropolis, Demand of the Government a speedy settlement of this question. Every hour of delay is big with risk. Remember, as Governor Boutwell suggests, that our present financial prosperity comes because we have corn to export in place of cotton; and that another year, should Europe have a good harvest and we an ordinary one, while an inflated currency tempts extravagance and large imports, general bankruptcy stares us in the face. Do you love the Union? Do you really think that on the other side of the Potomac are the natural brothers and customers of the manufacturing ingenuity of the North? I tell you, certain as fate, God has written the safety of that relation in the same scroll with Justice to the negro. The hour strikes. You may win him to your side; you may anticipate the South; you may save twelve million of customers. Delay it, let God grant McClellan victory, let God grant the stars and stripes over New Orleans, and it is too late.

Jeff Davis will then summon that same element to his side, and twelve million of customers are added to Lancashire and Lyons. Then commences a war of tariffs, embittered by that other war of angered nationalities, which are to hand this and the other Confederacy down for twenty-five or thirty years, divided, weakened, and bloody with intestine struggle. And what will be our character? I do not wholly agree with Edward Everett, in that very able and eloquent address which he delivered in Boston, in which, however, he said one thing pre-eminently true—he, the compromiser—that if, in 1830–31, nullification, under Jackson, had been hung instead of compromised, we never should have had Jeff Davis. [Loud applause.] I agree with him, and hope we shall make no second mistake of the kind. But I do not agree with him in the conclusion that these nineteen States, left alone, would be of necessity a second-rate power. No. I believe in brains; and I know these Northern men have more brains in their right hands than others have in their heads. [Laughter and cheers.] I know that we mix our soil with brains, and that, consequently, we are bound to conquer. Why, the waves of the ocean might as well rebel against our granite coast, or the wild bulls of the prairies against man, as either England or the South undertake to stop the march of the nineteen free States of this continent. [Applause.]

It is not power that we should lose, but it is character. How should we stand when Jeff Davis had turned that corner upon us—abolished slavery, won European sympathy, and established his confederacy? Bankrupt in character—outwitted in statesmanship. Our record would be, as we entered the sisterhood of nations, "Longed, and struggled, and begged to be admitted into the partnership of tyrants, and they were kicked out!" And the South would spring into the same arena, written on her brow, "She flung away what she thought gainful and honest, in order to gain her independence!" A record better than the gold of California or all the brains of the Yankee.

Righteousness is preservation. You who are not Abolitionists do not come to this question as I did—from an interest in these four million of black men. I came on this platform from sympathy with the negro. I acknowledge it. You come to this question from an idolatrous regard for the Constitution of '89. But here we stand. On the other side of the ocean is England, holding out, not I think a threat of war—I do not fear it—but holding out to the South the intimation of her willingness, if she will but change her garments, and make herself decent—[laughter]—to accept her under her care, and give her assistance and protection. There stands England, the most selfish and treacherous of modern governments. [Loud and long-continued cheers.] On the other side of the Potomac stands a statesmanship, urged by personal and selfish interests, that can not be matched, and between them they have but one object—it is in the end to divide the Union.

Hitherto the negro has been a hated question. The Union moved majestic on its path, and shut him out, eclipsing him from the sun of equality and happiness. He has changed his position to-day. He now stands between us and the sun of our safety and prosperity, and you and I are together on the same platform—the same plank—our object to save the institutions which our fathers planted. Save them in the service of justice, in the service of peace, in the service of liberty; and, in that service, demand of the Government at Washington that they shall mature and announce a purpose. That flag lowered at Sumter, that flight at Bull Run, will rankle in the heart of the Republic for centuries. Nothing will ever medicine that wound but the Government announcing to the world that it knows well whence came its trouble, and is determined to effect its cure, and, consecrating the banner to liberty, to plant it on the shores of the Gulf. [Applause.] I say in the service of the negro; but I do not forget the white man, the eight million of poor whites, thinking themselves our enemies, but who are really our friends. Their interests are identical with our own. An Alabama slaveholder, sitting with me a year or two ago, said:

"In our northern counties they are your friends. A man owns one slave or two slaves, and he eats with him, and sleeps in the same room (they have but one), as much as a hired man here eats with the farmer he serves. There is no difference. They are too poor to send their sons North for education. They have no newspapers, and they know nothing but what they are told by us. If you could get at them, they would be on your side, but we mean you never shall."

In Paris there are one hundred thousand men whom caricature or epigram can at any time raise to barricade the streets. Whose fault is it that such men exist? The Government's; and the Government under which such a mass of ignorance exists deserves to be barricaded. And the Government under which eight million of people exist, so ignorant that two thousand politicians and a hundred thousand aristocrats can pervert them into rebellion, deserves to be rebelled against. In the service of those men I mean, for one, to try to fulfill the pledge my fathers made when they said, "We will guarantee to every State a republican form of government." [Applause.] A privileged class, grown strong by the help and forbearance of the North, plots the establishment of aristocratic government in form as well as essence—conspires to rob the non-slaveholders of their civil rights. This is just the danger our national pledge was meant to meet. Our fathers' honor, national good faith, the cause of free institutions, the peace of the continent, bid us fulfill this pledge—insist in using the right it gives us to preserve the Union.

I mean to fulfill the pledge that free institutions shall be preserved in the several States, and I demand it of the Government. I would have them, therefore, announce to the world what they have never yet done. I do not wonder at the want of sympathy on the part of England with us. The South says, "I am fighting for slavery." The North says, "I am not fighting against it." Why should England interfere? The people have nothing on which to hang their sympathy.

I would have Government announce to the world that we understand the evil which has troubled our peace for seventy years, thwarting the natural tendency of our institutions, sending ruin along our wharves and through our workshops every ten years, poisoning the national conscience. We know well its character. But Democracy, unlike other governments, is strong enough to let evils work out their own death—strong enough to face them when they reveal their proportions. It was in this sublime consciousness of strength, not of weakness, that our fathers submitted to the well-known evil of slavery, and tolerated it until the viper we thought we could safely tread on, at the touch of disappointment, starts up a fiend whose stature reaches the sky. But our cheeks do not blanch. Democracy accepts the struggle. After this forbearance of three generations, confident that she has yet power to execute her will, she sends her proclamation down to the Gulf—Freedom to every man beneath the Stars, and death to every institution that disturbs our peace or threatens the future of our Republic. [Great applause followed the conclusion of the lecture.]

☞ *SEE NEXT PAGE.*

An important feature of the work is, that on controverted questions, whether involving constitutional principles or mere considerations of policy, the main arguments on both sides are impartially given, and submitted without comment to the judgment of the reader.

Subjoined to the work is an Appendix, containing

THE CONSTITUTION OF THE UNITED STATES;

A COPY OF THE ORIGINAL DRAFT OF THE

DECLARATION OF INDEPENDENCE,

showing what parts were struck out, and what were substituted and added by Congress;

THE ARTICLES OF CONFEDERATION,

and a statement of the Electoral Votes that have been given for the different candidates for President and Vice-President, from the first election of Washington, and the

NAMES OF ALL THE CABINET OFFICERS OF EACH ADMINISTRATION, ETC., ETC.

The work contains 1066 *pages, is well printed, on good paper, and very substantially bound in leather, and sold at the uniform price of* FOUR DOLLARS, BY TRAVELLING AGENTS, TO WHOM EXCLUSIVE TERRITORY IS GIVEN, *and of whom only it can be procured, as the work is not, nor will it be, for sale in bookstores.*

If, however, no Agent is accessible to those wanting the work, it will be supplied, free by express, or post-paid, on remitting the price to the Publisher,

N. C. MILLER,

25 Park Row, New York.

This book has received the strong recommendation of President Lincoln, the late Senator Douglas, and of most of the prominent Statesmen, Political Writers, and leading Editors of all parties in the United States, as an accurate history of the politics of our country.

www.ingramcontent.com/pod-product-compliance
Lightning Source LLC
LaVergne TN
LVHW011139110826
845150LV00008B/2421